"The whole is funny, grave and grand. Simply terrific."
—George Szirtes, author of Reel and The Burning of the Books

"It's a great, great book."
—Roddy Doyle, author of The Commitments and Paddy Clarke Ha Ha

"Stephens's pieces, particularly the personal ones, are hard-won, deeply honest and unaccommodatingly true. The 'Irishness' of the writing is of course not a matter of nativity or direct experience but of keen imagination and percipience."
—Richard Gilman, literary critic and scholar

SIXMILEBRIDGE

M. G. Stephens

SPUYTEN DUYVIL

NEW YORK CITY

SIGHTINGS

*Did you
hear*

the owl?

*That's a dove,
my love.*

Table of Contents: *Sixmilebridge*

I carry the sun in a golden cup,
The moon in a silver bag.
—W. B. Yeats

"It's all the same to morning what it dawns on—"
—Nuala Ni Dhomhnaill

"They had to reach the six-mile bridge."
—Zora Neale Hurston

"I am troubled, I'm dissatisfied, I'm Irish."
—Marianne Moore

Sixmilebridge

When you come to the fork in the road, take
It, Yogi Berra once said, and maybe

He had been to Sixmilebridge. When you come
To the bridge, take the high way, the left fork,

Not the right fork at the Y in the road.
That's because the place washed away in rains

Which would not, could not, did not stop pouring
Down a deluge upon this part of Clare.

The good news is that the high road is safe,
Lovely, a one-lane affair, with lots of

Turnoffs so that oncoming lorries and
Cars can navigate past without trouble.

It leads over the hill where you exit
Onto the old Broadford-Sixmilebridge road

Just before Dillon Motors, and Snata
Is a mile beyond that. But wear high boots.

Watch for fallen trees. Water's everywhere.

THE AUTOBIOGRAPHY OF MY FATHER

He was five years old, wandering alien
Streets in Brooklyn, his mother having just

Died and his father nowhere to be found,
The young boy walked around the world that way

Out in traffic of the borough until
Two of his County Mayo uncles found

Him wandering around, raggedy and
Dazed, and already hardened, suspicious,

Hungry, but he accepted their food as
Well as comfort and let them search the bars

Until they found the drunk, missing father,
Who didn't seem to know his son or them,

His brothers-in-law, until much later,
Sober, he asked them how his sick wife was.

The Butcher and the Cook

1. Joe the Butcher

Joe the Butcher talks about Descartes and
All of the life of the mind when he works

In the slaughterhouses of New Jersey
Or in the rare kitchens of the Palisades,

Severing arteries and boning chickens for
Meals at four-star hotels. Sometimes, when I

See Joe the Butcher, I am reminded
Of Prince Wen Hui's cook who practiced

The Tao of cutting up an ox, not just
By mass but by distinctions, as he said.

Finally, he saw nothing with his eyes.
The cleaver found its own way by instinct,

If not of the steel blade and wood handle,
Then the intuition of the butcher.

2. Prince Wen Hui's Cook

Other cooks needed a new cleaver once
A year when the blade became dull with hacks

Made at the sinews and bones from oxen.
Not Wen Hui's cook who had the same cleaver

For nineteen years. Cook slaughtered a thousand
Oxen with that Taoist cleaver, you know.

The secret: look for the spaces between
The joints. When tough joints came, he felt them, slowed

Down, sensed where an opening occurred, and
Went right for those sinews. Meat fell away

Like a plot of earth breaking in cracked hands.
He withdrew the blade from the ox. He let

Pleasure of the moment slip over him,
Wiping bloody cleaver on white apron.

St Stephens Day

A thousand starlings
Circle overhead all is

Still the moon out for the first
Time in thirty-seven years

On Christmas just past
Where are yesterday's snows

Where has the year gone
Where have the years gone

Portrait of the Artist as Francis Bacon

If you look closely at his paintings, see
How there is not a dot or blob, a blot

Or smudge out of place, a shape or a line
That's not working artistic overtime.

All is well on the canvas, even if
His studio was famous for its mess

And clutter, paint drips everywhere, paint
Cans and tubes of paint everywhere, too.

The painter drifted through, in drunkenness
And with clarity, seeing an order

That escaped everyone else, lovers
And dealers, pub friends and patrons alike.

The choice is one at which you have to guess:
He's mad, you might say, or a damn genius.

Oceanic: Bill of Lading

In her old age, stern as hell, she served us
Tea in dainty cups on saucers with spoons,

Stale cookies on the plate, she wore wire-rimmed
Glasses, and spoke in a thick brogue, almost

In a whisper, my father's relation,
Aunt Annie, from Sixmilebridge in County

Clare, just to the west of Limerick,
She came over on the Oceanic,

May 3, 1905, and cleared the way
For her brother (my grandfather), his bride,

And my father to come many years hence.
Silence was their way to communicate,

Exile was their modus operandi,
Cunning was how they got to stay so long.

THE GLASGOW KISS [1]

All day they drank pint after pint of stout,
And then they fell silent, two intense men

Brooding at the bar, until one of them
Whispered *Rangers*. The other said *Celtic*.

"Billshit," Roddy said. "You and yours are shite."
Martin countered that his friend's family

Were piss artists and tossers, his sisters
Just slags and degenerate beauty queens.

"Your mother is a plonker," the first one
Declared, "and your father's out on license."

"He's a good enough dad," Martin told him.
Then he leaned into his good friend quickly,

Smashing their skulls, foreheads clashing, bone-thump,
Blood-burst, Roddy's brains spilled out at the bar.

---

1 A Glasgow kiss is a British expression for a head-butt. Other region-
al expressions include the Croydon facelift, a tightly pulled ponytail,
and being sent to Coventry—being in the doghouse. Sending coals to
Newcastle is no longer as strange as it once was, though.

Irish Haiku

<u>15 – 27 April 1919</u>

Here's to Limerick
Soviet, fortnight of life
Lived at its extreme

<u>Lyra McKee</u>

"Derry tonight," she
Reported, it was her last—
"Absolute madness."

<u>A Little Irish</u>

Van Morrison, Dave
Van Ronk: a little

Irish goes a long way.
Billie. Ella. Tyson. Ali.

Her Dream

Red, one-eyed fox—
Dodder River, Dublin,
Locals call you Braveheart.
I call you brother.

Falconers

The eagle refuses to hear the call
From the falconer in a circle of

Freezing people there to learn falconry.
The field is sodden with winter, the mud

Everywhere amid the mizzling rain
And the December chill. A chick, yellow

Like the very sunshine, only dead as
A doornail, lay in the falconer's hand,

Leather-gloved to his elbow to protect
Him from the eagle's talons when it lands.

The sunshine is nowhere to be seen on
This gloomy afternoon in Bedfordshire,

Light slowly fading from the day, eagle
Still deciding whether to fly home or

Not, but hunger always rules this great beast,
So it tips off the post and glides under

A leafless beech tree and softly alights
Onto the extended arm of someone
26

As reluctant a falconer as bird
Is reluctant to participate in

The class on eagles and owls.
                              and far from

This sullen field a world at war, also
Reluctant to participate, goes on

And on with car bombs, suicide bombers,
Exploding boys and girls, babies, even

Old ladies exploding in the market,
All going up in smoke, far from this field,

The falconer and the reluctant ones,
The eagle and the would-be falconers.

After Forty

If she could recall that old song dancing
Around in her head when she was young and

So alive with pleasure for life, if only she
Could remember, she would see that as much

As it was good then, it is still good now,
And if she could sing, this is what she'd sing,

This song about her life, and how it is
Remarkable, and so she might tangle

And untangle those years until they were
Unknotted and smooth, almost as though years

Became seconds, unraveled like a skein,
Until she stood there in front of the hall

Mirror, clothed or naked didn't matter,
Neither old nor young, and yet beautiful,

In this predicament called life, if she
Could run or kick or scream, it would not make

One bit of difference to this quiet
Moment there with herself, and herself who
28

Accepts who that person is before her.

Missing Silverware

Phantoms annoy my memory palace
Late at night into early morning light,

Streeling through the halls like banshee, they sing
Dissonantly, and so claim to be me

Or my siblings or old friends and lovers,
Even to aping our gestures, taking

Our old dramas and monologues, twisting
Them around into new provocations.

In other venues in the memory
Palace, antique butlers and maids are dimmed

By senility, recalling nothing
Of past events in the ancient dining

Hall, claiming to have no memory of
The rococo world inside of these rooms.

The Smoke of Need

Is there anything more quiet than smoke,
Curling upwards like a spiral staircase

Leading to heaven? There is a quantum
Of smoke, its quorum, a mere transcription

Of its midnight ramblings, more silent than
Worry or desperation, it curls up.

Smoke has the right to remain silent or
Never say anything at all, it drifts

Upward, transfixed by its own gray machines
Of the night, if you try to engage it,

It floats away from you, but soaks itself
In the fabric of your shirt, your jacket,

Your scarf, it never wants to talk or be
A part of the conversation, choosing

The corners and the edges of most things,
Preferring its role as silent partner,

Contemplating the ozone of the night.
Smoke is as soft as the wind in shadows,

Its hand on your face, transparent as air.

A Rogue Wave

       Ocean gardening was the challenge, how
to make vegetables grow in the salt

air, or going the back road that led to
       Truro, searching out blueberry patches

that, like wild bears, we used to ravage with
our purple tongues, bringing home oysters by

       the bucketsful, freezing the pieces of
striped bass—not yet become contaminated—

and smoking bluefish to be eaten with
       olives and onions. All of these things broke

like a rogue wave over me as she stood
in the doorway talking about summer.

       Boston still lacked sunlight, and yet as I
walked to the T, the sky turned oystery.

PROVENÇAL

What we do with each other as lovers
Is no one's business but ours alone,

So it is all right to be here again,
So many years and lives later, here we

Are who we once were, young, alive and well,
Without even one care to burden us,

You and me, me and you, remembering
Convenient, forgetting inconvenient

Truths, so that even the lies are lovely,
Or maybe it is that only the lies

Were true beyond the bedroom's blue curtains
And council estate windows, and yet to

Be here now with you, to be here with each
Other, is a kind of incomparable

Bliss, there is no denying that neither
God nor the devil does harm to lovers.

Snata Was Not Cuchulain's Turf

Snata was not the land where Cuchulain
Learned to leap or go into warp spasms,

Nor did it have the drama of the Burren
Or the Cliffs of Moher to the west of there,

But rather was a bee-laden, cow-flop,
Muddy tract of land where cousin Jack stood

In the doorway of his cavelike dwelling,
Nose the size of a Chicago gangster's,

Scally cap on the right way, with crooked
Smile and bedazzled eyes, wearing purple

Shirt and stylish loafers in the muddy
Yard between house and barn, between us two

Two different worlds, and mine was that of
Selby's *Last Exit to Brooklyn*, Monk's mood.

Equal to the Equinox

There is probably an old jazz tune
That mirrors what I'm saying about the moon,

And the moon has already moved on,
Going from gibbous to full and back upon

Itself, reflecting what it is by the sun,
Suggesting that with my life, I've only just begun.

There is probably an old jazz tune
That mirrors what I'm saying about the moon.

Reading Moya Cannon

Her poems are mostly of light,
And the salt air, language, her own
And others, words slipping away
Like erosion off a cliff-face
That you see from a boat bobbing
In bitter sea off Donegal;
So it is the light which remains
In mind after you read one of
Her poems like "Little Skellig,"
Gannets flying about the boat,
Wind in your face all the way home.

The Vestibule

Nuala writes: "Is there a word for sex in
Irish, indeed! Is there an Eskimo

Word for snow?" And when I was a boy I
Once heard it said that the Irish had no

Word no word for no. But I come from across
The bitter sea, me and my brothers all

Brooklyn brutes and the sisters too they were
Ghetto goddesses like their freezing aunts

And their warm-hearted mother who told us
We were not Irish but American,

Not really gringos but New Yorkers, not
From Manhattan but Brooklyn. Yet the likes

Of what we used to hear in the parlor,
Down vestibules in battered old squalor!

Romantic Ireland Was Dead

Kids in nylon pants with white stripes down the
Side of the legs, scally caps on backwards

A la Samuel Jackson's black Kangol hat,
Everything was ass-backwards about

Them, almost like I had happened upon
A gang in Somerville, Mass or South Boston.

It was like being back in Brooklyn long
Ago or Hell's Kitchen in Manhattan

A few days earlier. We had stepped on
The set of a nasty rap song, the boys

Angry as rats in a dustbin disturbed
By dustmen cleaning the streets of refuse.

But romantic Ireland was dead and gone,
With old Yeats, Beckett, and Joyce in the grave.

What the Butler Saw: A Whodunit

If you please, if you will, sir, right this way.
Madame is under the weather, but she

Will be down shortly. His lordship is here,
But he is occupied at the moment.

The children and grandchildren are away,
Sir, I am working with a skeleton

Staff, just a maid, a cook and me.
If you please, if you will, sir, right this way.

Madame has had a fall, only a slight
Contusion on her forehead, some bumps and

Bruises on her arms and legs, but is well.
If you please, if you will, sir, right this way.

At the same time, sir, my lord hurt his hand
In the bathroom. If it is all right with

You, we'll let you wait here in this parlour.
If you don't mind, if you'd be so kind, sir.

I'll call the lady of the house for you.
I'll tell his lordship that you are now here.

If you'd be so kind, sir, if you don't mind.
If it is not an inconvenience,

Please wait in this parlour to the right here.
Have a seat. Have a cigar. May I park

Your car for you, may I offer a drink?
If you don't mind, if you'd be so kind, sir.

CRAZY SALAD

This mesclun, so colorful and healthy,
Reminds me of hallucinatory

Days of my youth when mescaline also
Was so colorful but so unhealthy,

At least, being crazy, it never helped
Me to understand myself or the world

Around me, but only bred a kind of
Insolent grandiosity fueled by

Low self-esteem and great paranoia.
Crazy, isn't it? It reminds me of

Listening to Van Morrison's "Crazy
Love" or reading Yeats' Crazy Jane poems.

This explains the violent moods, I said.
Or maybe it's something in the salad.

What Matters Is This

What remains when everything else is
Stripped away is what really matters, not

The things we thought so important, a way
To dress, a piece of music we had to

Have, a particular house or flat, some
Apartment in Paris or New York, books

Of one kind or another, not a few
But thousands of them everywhere, prints

And drawings, paintings and sculptures we thought
We could not live without, even certain

People we could not live without, all this
Didn't matter at the end of the day

Or the middle of the night, what matters
Is this, the two of us here together.

THE CULT OF ISAAC

We all know about Abraham, the great
Religions emanating from his skull,

But what about Isaac, where is his world
Taken into theological thought,

Mulled over by the great philosophers
Of the world, dissected and long discussed?

Isaac endured his god-thirsty father's
Knife and blood-fanatical intentions.

He was to be his father's sacrifice.
What I propose is Isaac, his worship

And adoration, a cult of the son.
In the cult of Isaac, there will be no

Worshipping of blood-lusting gods, only
Children and their safety and our great love.

Rembrandt Self-Portrait at Kenwood House

His obsession is to observe the world,
Particularly frail human nature,

Looking with kindness at all our foibles.
Yet don't forget his cold eye, weary yet

Compassionate, full of his scrutiny,
That compulsion to stare everyone

Into their elementary patterns.
He is a big, round man, thick hands and neck.

But everything seems to be going
Pear-shaped, his mid-section and his old life.

Gravity presses on him like a stone.
With his closest friends and associates,

Even family, his look is forlorn,
As if he were saying: Soon he'd be gone.

Kin Kindred Kind

Sixmilebridge was not the Aran Islands, and yet its rocky fences reminded me of it, an accordion of rocks stacked and religiously attended to, kine on the hill, kith in earth, grave and dead, craven me worshipping them here and now, stacking their corpses like they were found stones to make a fence with, progenitors, kin kindred kind of, forebears and ancestors, Jack's and mine, though we shed no tears for them because tears are not what we were taught to shed, even if it's taken years to come to this land of odd brethren, this land of breath and tongue, old syllables, so far off.

Laura's Dilemma

A couple shag
Noisily

In a Fiat 500
On her road

On the Heath
Broom and

Forsythia bloom
Finches sing

It must be Spring

Gospel Oak

The fight dog's name, said its proud owner, was
Jake, an old white bull terrier, brindle

Circle around his left eye, big splayed paws,
All about, he had nicks and healed red wounds

Because Jake got into tussles with male
Dogs he didn't like, pit bulls, Staffordshires,

Beat-up mongrels roaming council estates.
The owner of the white bull terrier

Was a young kid with half his teeth missing,
Tattoos on his arms and neck, in each ear

Earrings, loopy and large, gold rings every
Finger, he wore a dirty bandana

Around his neck, large cuts and little nicks
And scars in hands and throughout his shaved head.

Cognate

The world, at best, is dumb and beautiful,
At worst, an ugly mess. It knows nothing,

Is without a care, not being cogent,
Not even responsible for it all.

We humans, on the other hand, know just
About everything, and nothing at

All, yet ignorant or wise, it is we
Who are responsible to protect it.

The world, at best, is dumb and beautiful,
And we protect it from its predators,

Who are also us, so that we must be
Good cop and bad cop, or we will perish.

We humans, on the other hand, know just
Where the world is heading with us in charge,

And that appears to be our perishing,
Let me ask, where are we going right now?

WELLFLEET

What Mrs. Wilson told him back then was
That he was too young to be settling down—

Year-round life on Cape Cod—and that he should
Go back to the city to experience

The world, then maybe come back to Wellfleet
When he's fifty. And seeing this person

From Wellfleet brought back those old memories
Again, of how the sun and wind burn a

Kind of purity into the cheekbones,
How all your muscles and bones ache with health

And goodness from being outside all day,
The lungs filled with sea air, the hands nicked by

Fish hooks and oyster knives, hammering nails
And chopping wood, tending a garden plot.

THE IRISH WORD FOR SEX

At least these relations ate plain, boiled food
like potatoes and peas, corned beef, cabbage,

       parsnips and turnips, porridge oats, whiskey
and beer chasers, none of this spaghetti

and meatballs, flirting with the neighborhood
       mothers and daughters, or running numbers

rackets from the basement for the summer.
And even though there was a word for sex

       in Irish the Irish never said it,
that word or any other was not said

in our childish presences though even
       I, as unworldly as an angel, knew

there was some kind of shenanigans went
on to make babies, in any event.

Moments of the Moon

1. Sunlight Passes through Earth's Envelope

The Moon lies in front of the stars of the
Constellation Pisces, the Earth, Sun and

Moon in an almost exact line, but with
The Moon on the opposite side of the

Earth from the Sun, and as it moves into
The planet's shadow, it dims but still can

Be seen by sunlight passing through the Earth's
Atmosphere, but as light passes through its

Gaseous envelope, green to violet
Colors get filtered out, while red, it goes

On and on to the Moon, reaching the Moon's
Surface, allowing Earthlings to see this

Blood moon, and because the Moon's perigee
Is upon us, it is a supermoon.

2. Earth's Umbra

The Moon does not circle the Earth, but it
Takes an elliptical path, and while an

Eclipse can be charted to the second,
The supermoon is more fickle, more art

Than science, more the realm of poetry
Than mathematics, and of course the Moon's

Size is pure illusion, appearing much
Larger at horizon than in the sky,

And so the Moon enters Earth's penumbra,
And so becomes yellowy up there in

The heavens amid the stars, but two hours
Later enters the Earth's umbra, the inner

Dark corpus of the planet's own shadow,
And there I stood, alone, in the cold of

Night, 3:47 a.m., looking
At the Moon as it turned blood red above.

3. Blood Moon

Visions of Garcia Lorca fill up
The night, while outside the enormous Moon

Fills the sky, Earth's satellite, the domain
Of lovers, poets, lunatics, winos

And a woman pregnant with her first child;
Called blood because the blue light scatters off

The Moon's surface, but the red light, Robert
Johnson sang, was my mind, and that light stays.

I woke at all hours of the night, worried
That I might miss the lunar event in

London, so was outside at 2:30,
And then again at 3:30 a.m.,

The street empty, the night cold and so clear,
I heard fox prowling in the underbrush.

St Patricks Day

The moon is green with pearls, anemones
And metallic debris, Fender guitars,

Lug nuts, donuts, nutty sayings, prayers
For the dead back on Earth, phillips-

Head screws, electric toothbrushes, washers
From old dryers, canisters from old sky-

Lab astronauts, disgraced after falling
In love with their young Russian counterparts,

The first time this has happened, says TV
Anchorman, crestfallen over the news,

This idea of orbiting space stations
Filled with cosmonauts in love or worse yet,

Having sex as their space station orbits
The Earth, so high up, on St Patrick's Day.

Her Gray-Green Eyes

Because I am the luckiest person
Alive—after all, I am in love with

You, and you return the favor being
In love with me—I am the luckiest

Person in the world—after all, I am
In love with, et cetera, the object

Of my affection, subject of this tale,
This lover's discourse, of course, keeping in

Mind, too, that I am, in turn, turned into
Both subject and object of desire in

Your eyes, et cetera, et cetera—
Did I say gray? For they are a gray-green,

A blue of stone, a green of tea, a gray
Of rolling sky in winter reverie.

Epithalamium

Waking to city roses and lilies,
Blue silk ribbons, color of corn flowers,

The scaly trout and greedy pike all jump
For joy in late June, first days of summer,

A perfect kind of day for these lovers
To nuptualize and romanticize, bid

All come forth to celebrate, deer and wolves,
Lark singing in the summery green trees,

And even the owl's shrill call turns mellow
And seems to warble, for the dew on ground,

Humidity in the air, even rain
Cannot dampen their spirits, nor deter

Them from their purpose to be together,
And then to make a life with each other.

Knockout

As I walked
Through

Knocknaheeney
(Cnoc na hAoine),

I was thinking
Of

Seamus Heaney,
Only I wound

Up in
Gurranabraher

(Garran na mBrathar)
Where

I ran into
(I swear to

God)
My grandmother

Montreal

We had driven north out of Boston and
West into the afternoon and again

North going across the border into
Canada, listening to a tape from

A friend's wedding in Somerville the year
Before: Earth, Wind and Fire (on and on and

On), KC and the Sunshine Band (do a
Little dance, make a little love, get down

Tonight). Today so many years have passed
By, who knows where the friend is nowadays,

But we still have each other, though we have
Not been to Montreal since that long gone

Trip: *boules* of coffee, hot fresh bread, the cold.
I remember your beautiful face there.

CHUM

They can cut the chum, but it doesn't mean
That I have to take the bait. It was an

Expression that people from Brooklyn and
Long Island used, speaking about being

Drawn into a debate or argument
That they didn't want to be drawn into.

Chum was a bloody stew of fish (entrails,
Liver, other giblets) that were cast out

Upon the water to draw larger fish
Or sharks to its red sea of mess and guts.

I have to recall that saying when some
People try to draw me into crazy-

Making attacks for no good reason. They
Can cut chum; I don't need to take the bait.

Easter 2016

One hundred years ago, their Irish blood
Spilled all over O'Connell Street, people

Mowed down near the General Post Office,
Dead horses in the side roads, Phoenix Park,

Dead citizens on the dank Dublin streets.
Now everyone just strolls past Bewley's

Without a care in the world except to
Ask what's at the cinema, what's on the

Telly, whose band is rocking Temple Bar?
If the ghosts of 1916 roamed here,

They would not recognize the terrible
Beauty of this island, only the rough

Beast that comes 'round, making the spectres ask:
For what purpose did they shed so much blood?

Freud's Nudes

Art is long, but gravity is deeper,
Always pulling us downward to our end,

Only it takes a Lucian Freud to note
Our journey in all its fallen details.

Afterward, you venture through the city,
Observing the blotchy reds, the pinkish

Welts, the pale, veiny arms and throats,
The whiteness of their bones, and then go home.

Flesh fails, ineluctably pulling us
Downward, is our undoing, while undressing

Is just taking off our clothes, and being
Naked is a state of extremity,

Cradle to the grave, but being nude is
How the artist sees us as an ideal.[2]

---

2 Flesh betrays us not only by our sins, but by gravity
pulling us earthward. Look at those fleshpots of humanity in
Lucian Freud's paintings. Was there ever artist who showed
humankind so bluntly? Think of pink cherubs in Rubens,
darkness all around the flesh in Rembrandt, creatures almost

Love is What We Need

What someone might call expediency,
We call by other names, words in the night

Whispered across tangled sheets, sweat, and
Sleep, wound around each other like ribbons

Or human shrouds, yet love is what we call
It because love is what we really need,

Or call it lust by any other name,
Salty, unambiguous, full of smells

In the night, vanilla, rose, lavender,
Rosemary, bergamot, eucalyptus,

Camphor, thyme, patchouli oil, the bedroom
Closed to the outside world, no lights, no air,

Only each other, whispering across
The sheets and the night, I love you, you say,

---

too beautiful (Degas, Matisse, or Bonnard). It is not a lie to see
the world so ideally, only it is just that alone, an ideal. Freud's
flesh is everyday real, paint full of gravity, pulling itself down-
ward to the final end, his cremnity white end of it all.

And I answer that I love you too, words,
Words, words, said like a mantra, over and

Over, as if repetition would make
Them true, when the only thing honest and

True were ourselves naked under the sheets,
And that was always true, even if we

Sometimes didn't believe anything else.

THREE POEMS FOR KENN MILLER[3]

1. A Kestrel Suite

For lunch I make a pasta of penne,
Tomato sauce, mixed olives, ciabatta,

And a tossed green salad, no meat, no cheese.
But as the water boils and the sauce cooks

I hear a screech, a cry from the alley,
And I go to the kitchen door to see

What the commotion is all about, and
I look at bird and bird looks back at me.

At the kitchen door, a kestrel, yellow
Eyes intently staring at me inside,

Pins a screeching bird to the ground outside.
The starling cries out, but its life slowly

Drains in a pool of blood under raptor.
The kestrel delights at its own dinner.

---

3 Miller is the author of *Tiger the Lurp Dog*, one of the best novels about
the Vietnam War. A skilled linguist, especially with Chinese, he served as
a Lurp (long-range reconnaissance patrols) in the U. S. Army. Kenn has
long believed that corvids are the most intelligent form of life on Earth.

2. Kestrel on Thermals

I saw a raptor descend from a cloud
Over the Heath and hover on the hill

Above the playing field near the playground
And the running track below Parliament

Hill; hover and strike down upon its prey,
A field mouse whose color of urine gave

It away to the slow-gliding bird on
The thermals, breaking through the loft of air,

Diving toward the ground cover between
Field and hill, hovering feet from the ground,

Then sinking its deadly talons into
The mouse. I watched it envelop the mouse,

Devour it alive, this rusty kestrel,
Its movement so graceful, so orchestral.

3. Two Crows and a Kestrel

A hundred feet up, south of Parliament
Hill, a kestrel hovers above its prey.

Then two crows fly toward it, first one then
The other bumps it, midair, feathers fly,

And instead of fighting crows, the kestrel
Moves on as the pair dance in autumn air,

Kings of Parliament Hill, kings of Hampstead
Heath, even Camden and beyond, London

North of Euston, and all the way toward
Its northernmost borders, birds of the world,

You better watch your sorry, feathery
Asses 'cause the crows are rulers of sky

Above and grass below, the hill and bush,
The open grassy fields, and all—they rule!

Walking City to City

It occurs to me that I have spent most of life
Walking aimlessly from one place to another

Not in the natural world but the built world of
Cities sometimes going from one to another

Then zigzagging around them street to street walking
Everywhere I went not briskly but saunter

Was my pace and my speed resembled the turtle's
Or even the snail or sometimes even the slug

So that all my life was a walk never a run
Stopping to look to taste to see I listened to

Everything I saw curiosity was
My gift I wore like a colorful scarf around

My neck good legs the gift that propelled me along
Poverty being yet another gift I used

Like a companion in this long journey through life
I never fit in was still another great gift

Being the outsider forever looking and
Looking in the window at things I couldn't ever
68

Have until I learned to not want them a love of
People places and things what drove me onwards to

The next street the next place or the next city or
The next one the next one someone who understood

Or seemed to know the way to yet another place

Love Poem #472

I want to be like the rain on flowers
(Echinacea, delphinium, or corn

Flowers, even wild flowers, wild for the
Taking), I want to be water to your

Thirst, I want to be with you on this earth,
Right this moment, as we are, with no thought

Towards invention, no pretense about
Deceit, no blathering about love, so

Much as love being our actions, a trust,
An example, doing these things together,

Such as taking walks, making pesto,
Discussing ideas late into the night,

Sun coming up through the bedroom windows,
Turning this love poem into an aubade.

Housesitting

This house of wood and nails and love and pain,
This house of rice and bread and oil and eggs,

Of jam and tears and cheese and red onions,
Of blinds and chairs and tables and rules and cares,

This house of trees and bricks and bugs and rulers,
Of barbecues, Suzy Q's, Q-tips, bikes,

Of books, manuscripts and notebooks, more books,
And even more, this house of spirit, sprites,

Earthly delights, wild nights, calm days, after-
Noons under the trees in the backyard shade,

This house of wood floors, of showers and towels,
Of oatmeal and dry cereal and toast,

Coffee in the morning, coffee in June,
This house of drama and love at noon.

The Bicyclist

The traffic sets like a stalled game of chess,
Cars packed one behind the other, horns honk,

Drivers shout profanities, but nothing
Moves, congestion everywhere, sirens

Go off, tempers flare up. It has just gone
Four o'clock on a Thursday afternoon,

Smog settles over the city, gray and still,
The Thames moments away, Monet-like.

Into this clot in the artery of
The city comes a bicyclist, green

And red and yellow and even orange
On his jacket and shorts, helmet on head,

He sings a song, top of his lungs, alive,
Alive, he is nothing but that, and well.

Boxing

1.
Mike you dirty Irish bastard
He would say when he called me

On the telephone
To see when we could hang out

And he would come to my flat
On 110th Street in Morningside Heights

Where I made him a tuna fish
Sandwich and we watched old fights

He was Billy Graham
Irish Billy Graham a welterweight

They called him to distinguish
Him from the evangelist

And Billy once told me a story
About a fight he had in the

Coney Island Velodrome
Losing every round

Because he wouldn't listen
To his cornerman and trainer

Whitey Bimstein who told him
To move to the right or left

In order to stop being hit
By his opponent but Billy

Balked and didn't listen
And stood there slugging it out

2.
Just move to the right Whitey pleaded
Move a fuckin' inch to the right

So that this bastard will stop
Punching the shit out of you

But Billy being a stubborn Irishman
(his father Pop Graham was Scottish

And his mother came from Limerick)
Refused to budge for his opponent

And yet Billy went out there in the
Seventh round moved an inch to the right

Threw a left hook and knocked
Out this sorry-ass story of an opponent

And in Billy's corner Whitey Bimstein
Danced a jig that his fighter

Finally listened to the advice
And knocked out the bum

The moral of the story Billy asked me
The moral of the story

Then he laughed and said
How the fuck should I know

Leda's Advice to Her Observers

"I was fucked by a swan," she said matter
Of factly, and as young as she was, her

Green eyes contained a deadness residing
There, her long tendrils of hair specked with swan's

Down and feathers, fallen leaves and brown twigs
Matted into her clothes, her voice, hard and

Low, gravelly and firm, she lit up a
Cigarette and stared off in the distance.

"I am part of that god-damned group known as
Me Too," she told us observers in a

Conspiratorial way, she said, "If
It can happen to me, it can happen

To any one of you ladies, rich or
Poor, it could happen to anyone here."

His Voice, and How He Lost It

I'm over here in Berlin, trying to
Help Bono find his voice, has anyone

Seen it anywhere? Apparently he
Discovered it missing in the middle

Of a song onstage at a big concert,
So, please, we would ask you to be on the

Lookout for that unique Celtic item,
His raspy brogue, blues ridden, a bit of

Dublin there in the web of its details.
He may have lost it just about any-

Where in the city, a bus, a cab, train
Station, buying cigarettes from a kiosk,

The hotel where he was staying or on
The way to the performance venue or

Backstage in the green room before going
On or on the way to the stage,

and though

Eye-witness accounts vary, most agree

That it was apparent, mid-song, he had
No voice with which to finish his actions.

Yet however it happened, now it's lost,
So if you do find it, please be careful

About how you approach it, a singing
Voice being both resilient and also,

Like any talent, so amazingly
Fragile, determined and a bit wary

Of life or even the music business.

Spring

1.
Some time
In the
Spring term

I spring to
Life and
All is well

2.
Sometimes
In the
Springtime

I come to
Terms with
My time here

PIED BEAUTY

The long summer ends, and slowly autumn
Creeps over the horizon, one turned leaf

At a time, one fallen leaf a minute,
The days gradually wane, the blue night

Approaches its apex, and a blackness
Replaces the sunlight we took lightly,

Even for granted, when the birds were out
And about everywhere, and so free.

The light of October is red and green,
Yellow and slant, like a poem often

Is in the hands of our own Emily
Dickinson or maybe intensely said

In the lyrical mode of Gerard Manley
Hopkins, a family name, by the way.

Mingus at the Five Spot

I heard Mingus at the Five Spot Café
After it moved from the Bowery to

The corner at St. Marks Place, hot summer
Night, I was with my oldest brother James,

He then called himself, though I had known him
All my life as Jimmy. He was going

Through a brilliant manic phase of his life,
And stayed as a guest at my East 10th Street

Apartment just around the corner, and
Mingus, in a surly mood, removed cats

From his band who weren't carrying their
Loads, then he asked audience members to

Leave, but he overlooked my big, loud bro',
Claiming we all were more appreciative.

March 17, 1967

One St. Patrick's Day, I walked into a
Dusky Greenwich Village pub and was stopped

At the door by a doorman who said it
Was an Irish pub, so maybe I should

Go somewhere else for a drink. I was tall
And dark and I had a black goatee, long

Kinky black hair and a big broken nose
Fighting with everyone in the world.

I told this fellow where to go in so
Many words as I walked up to the bar

And ordered a drink, the doorman still by
The door wondering who I was coming

Into the pub like that, not realizing
He'd just met the most Irish person there.

Dempsey's / Times Square

1.
It's 1927, Chicago:
The stock market's simply going crazy,

And Jack Dempsey is fighting Gene Tunney.
With two huge shots to the head, Tunney goes

Down, but Dempsey forgets to go to the
Neutral corner, so the referee does

Not start counting for four seconds, leaving
The battered fighting Marine time to clear

His head, and by the Eighth Round, Dempsey
Uncharacteristically goes down,

Leaving Gene Tunney enough room to win
The fight, and afterwards both fighters walk

Away with bags and bags of money; they
Rolled in it until the Great Depression.

2.
My father knows Jack Dempsey and hangs out
In his restaurant and bar after work

Down the piers in Hell's Kitchen, and once in
A great while, he would gather his six sons,

Take us to Dempsey's for a meal, to meet
And greet the great boxing legend, his huge

Right hand reaching down to shake mine; I smelled
The stink of his beer and onion breath, which

Made me nauseous and dizzy, his craggy
Fighter's face smiling at me as he shouts

To a waiter to seat us at a big
Table where we eat marbled steaks and mashed

New potatoes, the great fighter bringing
Out plate on plate of his famous cheesecake.

3.
The sisters did not meet Jack Dempsey, but
Instead went out to lunch with grandmother,

The proper one, not the bawdy Irish
Dame we called grandma, but really was not

Any relation to any of us,
Being my father's stepmother, and his

Opposite, not to mention nemesis.
No, the girls got to go to lunch at Schraft's,

Ordering tuna fish sandwiches on
White bread with the crusts cut off, tasteless as

The dark décor, while their brothers got to
Walk around Times Square and Broadway, big shots

Like their father, who knew the prize fighter
Well enough not to need pay for their meals.

4.

Even at that young age, I'd ask myself,
Sitting at the table eating giant

Pieces of Jack Dempsey's famous cheesecake,
How come my father, whenever he took

Us out for a meal, he never seemed to
Pay the bill, even Dempsey telling him,

"It's on the arm," he said, "on me, the house."
So all the old man had to lay out for

Was the tip for the waiters, and being
Grandiose, although also a tight-wad

And a cheapskate, he left a twenty on
The table, with Dempsey insisting that

The old man was his friend and didn't have
To leave anything, what with all these kids.

5.

My mother—our mother—was sat at home
Reading the *Daily News* at the dining

Room table, drinking cheap red wine, smoking
Her Salem cigarettes, and living on

Entemann's cakes and black coffee, though by
Late afternoon, along with the wine, she

Drank a pot of Lipton's tea, getting out
The bone china cups and the old teapot,

Grateful for the quiet in her other-
Wise noisy house filled with children and more

Children, her own and her siblings', her own
And the stray neighborhood child without home.

Jack Dempsey? She had heard of him, but for
The life of her, could not put face to name.

Last Call on the First Cause

The world is not at all a certainty,
But a series of brilliant mishaps, chance

Encounters in the universe, our world
Come into being the result of things

Exploding outward, and the first effect,
Carbon, is a gift derived from actions

The by-product of—
                              do you see where this

Leads us, not so much to the feet of god
As to the doorstep of science, and that

What we humans know is limited to
Our emotions, our brains, our five senses,

Which lack a wide dimension to take in
The ineffable, our lives not broadly

Enough compassed to embrace beginnings
Or endings, which suggests that our world is

Not a mystery but a conundrum.

Bridget's Spring

Somewhere in moving from pagan goddess
To sainted mother of the hearth, Bridget

Was de-fanged, air-brushed, and cleaned up cheery
And without her green edge of the round earth,

They took away her sex, neutered her light,
Removed the smell of mulch and of peat bog,

Covered her breasts and round ass with clothes,
Now toothless and goddess of the gray hearth,

Of brooms and pots and little babies who
Ran about the house in poop-filled nappies.

Oh, Bridget we love you, get out of the
Kitchen and get back to the woods, the smell

Of rotting leaves and deer scat, rotten logs
And fallen trees, streams running with salmon.

Standing Eight Count

After one-hundred-and-ten fights, over
Eighty by knockout, only four losses,

One no-contest, and a draw, he was now
Punch-drunk and dopy, his twitch muscles all

But gone, and he keeps hearing bells go off
In his head, even amid the silence

Of the late afternoon, just him and the
Cat present in the apartment, his wife

Out doing errands; he saw himself come
Out of his corner, ready to do battle

Once more. Ali told it best when he said:
A fighter has only so many fights

In him or herself. Once s/he hits that number:
We know what that looks like afterwards.

Late November: 1963

I was 17 years old and going
To a state teachers college in upstate

New York, snow already falling, but gone
In an instant melt. The scent in the air

Was autumnal, the hills still full of fall's
Colors. There was a chill everywhere.

Church bells rang out and children played in front
Of the lab school, waiting for rides back home.

I walked lazily across the quad when
I saw a young woman run frantically

Towards me and then throw herself into
My arms, as she wept uncontrollably,

Finally saying, "The president, he's
Been shot." She then said: "He is dead. He's dead."

GREENBELT

My older brothers were back in Brooklyn.
Our father still worked as a chief petty

Officer in Naval Intelligence,
Stationed in Washington, D.C., mother

Just back from giving birth to me, her third
Child, another boy—her first girl not due

For two more years. We were children in a
Long line that would reach to sixteen of us.

I was like an only child growing up
By myself in Greenbelt, my mother's love

And attention a balm to my spirits.
I was the tallest baby, at the time,

Born in Washington, they said, twenty-seven
Inches long, while my mother was five feet

Two inches tall, and my father was just
Several inches taller than his wife.

She was a typical Greenbelt housewife,
While her husband was a typical worker bee

In the hive of U.S. intelligence,
The war winding down, but there was, he said,

More mopping up to do before they could
Return to Brooklyn and their two oldest

Boys. The story about the old man was
That he came home drunk one warm evening,

And fell immediately asleep on
The couch, only to be awakened by

A strange woman screaming bloody hell, so
He got up and left the apartment and

Went looking for his own similar one
Just down the road from where he had passed out

The night before. Then there was the time that
He left his drunken father in a bar

On Flatlands Avenue in Brooklyn, and
Instead chose the soberest Irishman

In the place, taking him across the road
To meet his future mother and father-

In-law, only my grandmother figured
Out right away what was going on and

Threw out the impostor and their daughter's
Wavy black haired fiancé, and the two

Went back to drink the night away in the
Little bar across the road. Ah, but that—

That is another story completely.

Grim's Bar

It was Grim the father who said that his
Son was one of the greatest ballplayers
In the world, and my Aunt Katherine—
The loud, drunk redhead at the end of bar,
Shouting for another fucking drink—Grim,
Come on, man, get with it, and besides, she
Said, your son is good, he's on the Yankees
After all, but the greatest in the world?
Katherine went on, they don't even play
Baseball in Ireland, for Crissakes, now give
Me another drink before I lose my
Temper and have you regret not serving
Your customers properly, the way you
Should be treating us on this lovely night.

THE SEAFARER

Went down to the West Side of Manhattan,
Hell's Kitchen, through it I walked lonely as
A teenager, which I was, 19 years,
And bounding towards Pier 90, noon hour,
I was told at the Union Hall, Seventh
Avenue, they said not to show up for
Work before that, and there I was on deck,
Ship bound east under Verrazano Bridge,
Threading the needle through the Narrows, sea-
Going, Atlantic Ocean before me,
The crew went back down below to do work
In the main galley or, in my case, crew
Mess, the sea, the sea, all around the ship,
Gigantic in New York harbor, but small
And vulnerable upon the waves and
Chop, and myself a combination of
Fear (did not know how to swim, though god
Knew going overboard this far from land,
Your chances were slim to survival), and
Out on my first great adventure in life,
Half the crew crazy and the other half
Stoned on alcohol and drugs, the passage
Ways redolent with marijuana and
The sweet, stinky smell of opium smoke,

Wafting down the below-sea-level space,
The crew quarters, between the hours when we
Worked our various two-hours on two-hours
Off shifts from six in the morning until
Close to midnight, day after day at sea,
Our first break coming when we hit the Mid-
Atlantic juncture of the Azores, and
Then only a few days more before we
Arrived at the North African port of
Casablanca, from there the night journey
To Algeciras, Gibraltar before
Us, monkeys scurrying over the Rock,
Set sail again, Palma de Majorca,
Genoa, Naples, then westward at night,
The next day Nice and Cannes, sleek speed boats there
To ferry crew and passengers back and
Forth until evening came down from Alps,
And we set out again, this time off coast
Of Africa, Funchal, Madeira, night
Again, and once again steaming westward,
Nantucket, Coney Island jellyfish,
We knew from the sight and smell of it, New
York, and gloaming city, was only beats
Away on pulse or clock, 21 days,
And we were back, Hudson River, the noise
And smoke, the smog and roar, Pier 90, home.

FORM AND FUNCTION

In the application for this mission,
They asked: "Who should we contact in case you
Become a martyr?" When I became a
Martyr to poetry, I filled out such
A form. But then I was rejected for
Having flat feet. Am I still a martyr,
If not to poetry, then to its Muse,
Which is love, always and forever still?
I am just another iambic-struck,
Love-belching fool whose ravings sometimes seem
To be poetry, even if there is
No rhyme or reason, no after aching
Climax and resolution, just these words
On the page that occasionally get
Spoken aloud in front of a crowd of
Poetry-loving fanatics nearby.
In my application for poetry,
I informed them that if I become a
Martyr, they should contact my late mother,
My late high-school writing teacher, and just
To be on the safe side, either Dante
Alighieri or Walt Whitman,
Though if they can skip the seventy-two
Virgins, I would prefer lunch in Zurich

With James Joyce, who I thought understood this
Idea of being a martyr better
Than anyone else, including Jesus.

The Pogues

There is something so refreshing
About Shane MacGowan's rotten
Teeth and dopy smile, eyes
In his head spinning out cartwheels
As he sings "Dirty Old Town" or
"Fairytale of New York," weather
Always grey and raining outside,
While in the pub, music rings in
My ears and rings out upon us
In the fallen world, hope something
That never interested us
Sort of people interested
In good craic and skipping the Mass,
Going out and having a gas.

Irish Eyes

These women, these moments, these trees, these things—
Flowers (irises), this eye's iris (a

Flower), this hour has a power to it
We walk in the emptied-tree splendor of

Winter: the light splinters through branches and clouds—
The loud is not very loud, but even

The wind has a say of what is allowed
And what is not aloud, but is silent.

The Irish have a word for this,
But I don't speak Irish.

Dirge for My Mother

I sit in a dive on the Kilburn High Road in West London, grieving for your passing; you had been alive, then you were dying, now you are dead. You are a world away in Florida, ashes to ashes already, as I pretend it will never be the case with me, your third son. A sister said I was a phony because I didn't actually care for you at the end of your life, and at the end of the day, she and the other sisters did. Those sisters fought like cats to prove their love for you was superior to all others who loved you from afar, and they fought with each other, too. My love is only that of a third child, one ocean removed, and you had so many children, both ingrate and loving, from near and from far. I suppose like so much in my life, I am like one of your gazelles, one of your zebras, wary and watching the lions eat your children at the edge of the pack—read here drugs and alcohol—and then turkey vultures descend from the sky to pick their bones. But the thing is, you were the best mother any of us had, earthy and real, a sober beauty until the very end. Even before your last breath, one of your feuding daughters applied lip gloss to your parched lips Even dead, you were given lipstick to wear by another passionate daughter dutifully attending to your last appearance. Finally all of this is about mothers and daughters, and sons are merely superfluous, even obscenities in this grief, in the death of a simple, kind woman. I was one of her six sons and three daughters, not counting seven other children no longer here to mourn her. Those other children all went somewhere far away, and not of this world, spirits of the realm, ghosting the universe. My mother is with them, and among the ancestors.

Acknowledgments

Some of these poems have appeared in the following magazines and journals:

Ploughshares
PN Review (U.K.)
Talisman
Gargoyle
Blood, Sweat and Ink (U.K.)
Cimarron Review
Hanging Loose
London Magazine (U.K.)
Poetic Matrix
Exquisite Corpse
Auk Contraire
Sport Literate
Poeming Pigeon
Uncensored Songs
Let Us Rise – An Anthology Commemorating the Limerick Soviet 1919
Spit Poet Zine
Bosphorus Review
Harbinger Asylum
Trouvaille Review
Rat's Ass Review

M. G. Stephens (Michael Gregory Stephens) is author of over 30 books, including two recent novels with Spuyten Duyvil, *King Ezra*, about the flawed Modernist genius Ezra Pound, and *Kid Coole*, the third book in *The Coole Trilogy*, the other books being *The Brooklyn Book of the Dead* and *Season at Coole*, the latter which E. P. Dutton published more than fifty years ago. Stephens was born in Washington, D.C., and grew up in Bedford-Stuyvesant, Brooklyn, and further out on Long Island, the third of sixteen children to an Irish gypsy father and a multiracial American mother from a family which traced its origins back to a slave owned by the Wheelock family, the founders of Dartmouth College. His play *Our Father* ran for over five years on Theatre Row (42nd Street), and has been produced several times in London, Chicago, and Los Angeles. He received his degrees after the age of 30 from the City College of New York, Yale University, and much later in life (60 years old), from the University of Essex in Colchester, England. Stephens lived in London for 15 years, mainly working in fringe theatres as a writer, director and actor, moving back to the U.S. just before the Covid-19 pandemic. He has both Irish and U.S. citizenships, and is anxious to travel again after being housebound with the rest of the country during the pandemic. He dreams of taking the night boat from Algeciras to Tangier and settling permanently in Northern Africa. Barring that he would settle for a winterized cottage on Cape Cod or at the end of Long Island.

9 781959 556695